A Plunder of Pirates

Scoular Anderson

Puffin Books

PUFFIN BOOKS

Published by the Penguin Group
Penguin Books Ltd, 27 Wrights Lane, London W8 5TZ, England
Penguin Books USA Inc., 375 Hudson Street, New York, New York 10014, USA
Penguin Books Australia Ltd, Ringwood, Victoria, Australia
Penguin Books Canada Ltd, 10 Alcorn Avenue, Toronto, Ontario, Canada M4V 3B2
Penguin Books (NZ) Ltd, 182–190 Wairau Road, Auckland 10, New Zealand

Penguin Books Ltd, Registered Offices: Harmondsworth, Middlesex, England

First published 1989
10 9 8 7 6 5 4 3 2

Text and illustrations copyright © Scoular Anderson, 1989

Printed in England by Clays Ltd, St Ives plc

CONTENTS

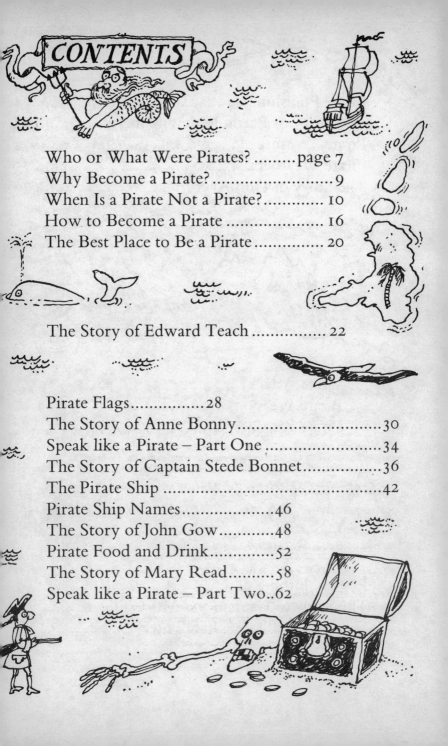

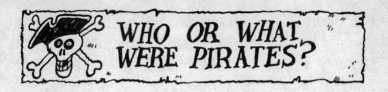

WHO OR WHAT WERE PIRATES?

Pirates were sea-robbers. They were gangs of lawless men – and women – who attacked ships in the hope of finding riches among the cargo.

There have probably always been pirates sailing the oceans of the world. The ancient Greeks were troubled by them. There are still pirates today. In the seas of the Far East they use fast, inflatable boats to attack unsuspecting ships.

However, the most important pirates, who were of all nationalities, lived during the sixteenth, seventeenth and eighteenth centuries. After North and South America had been discovered, many ships made the long and dangerous voyage from the Americas to Europe. Their holds were filled with plenty of tempting goodies, all worth stealing.

Sometimes the pirates would be lucky. There would be valuable items on board: gold, chests of money, precious stones. Even if there was little of such treasure, the pirate crew could always sell the rest of the cargo – perhaps silks or cattle or timber.

The pirates were mostly tough, rowdy, brutal and mercilessly cruel. Though perhaps they had one little soft dream in the back of their minds! They wanted to become rich as quickly as possible so they could go back home and settle down. They wanted a nice little house on shore with a few chickens scratching in the yard.

Not many of them made it. A life of violence usually ended in violence. There were not many pirates who died in their beds.

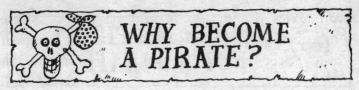

WHY BECOME A PIRATE?

Daily life was pretty harsh for ordinary people and certainly no fun. Some of them leapt at the chance of getting away from the dreary routine of scraping a living. Others were attracted by the idea of an exciting and adventurous piratical life (plus a little extra money on the side).

LIFE AT HOME
Plagues
Fevers and Fluxes
Starvation
Slums
Hard work on the land
Hard work in town
Harsh Laws
Harsh Punishment
Poverty etc etc etc...

LIFE IN PIRACY
Freedom
Adventure
Fresh Air
Wealth

(not to mention plagues, fevers, fluxes, scurvy, starvation, drowning, hanging, quartering, etc, etc, etc...)

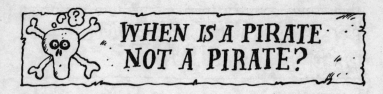

WHEN IS A PIRATE NOT A PIRATE?

There were three types of sea-robber. They were usually looked upon as pirates, but they didn't all call themselves by that name.

There were:

Buccaneers,

who attacked most ships but not usually those of

their own country (perhaps because they had a patriotic streak in them!).

Pirates,

who attacked any ship they came across, including those of their own country.

Privateers,

who were given permission by their government back home to attack and rob enemy ships.

Buccaneers: how they got their name

In the Caribbean Sea there were many islands which were paradise compared with other countries. The climate was fine, and there was food in plenty.

Many sailors and outcasts soon found these islands ideal places to live. They led a rough life but a good one. They ate fruit from the trees and hunted the wild pigs. They cooked or smoked the meat over an open fire on grills made of green twigs – a bit like barbecues. These grills were known by their French name: *boucans*. So the men became known as boucaniers or buccaneers.

Privateers (from the word "private")

Some captains with privately owned vessels were given permission by their governments to attack ships belonging to an enemy country.

For instance, the government of England gave permission for privateers to attack Spanish ships because the two countries were so often at war with one another.

Sir Francis Drake, although famous for his voyage around the world and his defeat of the Spanish Armada, was also a privateer. Many of his voyages were spent in attacking Spanish ships and relieving them of their precious cargoes.

Documents called 'letters of marque' were given to privateers by their governments. These letters gave them permission to attack enemy ships.

However, many of these letters were forgeries and were worthless. One captain sailed around the Caribbean Sea plundering as fast as he could because he claimed he had a letter of marque given to him by the Governor of the Danish West Indies. The letter was on the best parchment and decorated with fancy scrolls. As few people could read Danish they didn't know that the letter said only that the captain had the right to hunt pigs and goats on the islands.

Which leaves us with pirates – they're the *nasty* ones who would attack anyone!

Pirates received no wages, but they could share in any treasure found and spend it as they wished. There are a lot of adventurous tales about buried treasure and treasure maps. In truth, few pirates buried their treasure. Money buried under the ground was useless to pirates. It was far better in their pockets, where it could be spent on drinking and gambling. (Besides, there was the danger that other pirates might find buried treasure.)

Piracy offered freedom from all the many rules that guided daily life (having to pay taxes, for instance, or raise your hat to the lord of the manor). Things were not totally lawless on board ship, however. Pirate crews often drew up lists of simple rules that would prevent quarrelling or fighting from breaking out.

These rules were known as 'articles'. Here are some of the articles drawn up by the pirate crew of Captain John Phillips.

1 Every man shall obey civil command.

2 The captain shall have one full share and a half of all the prizes. The master, carpenter, boatswain and gunner shall have one share and one quarter. Each man of the crew shall have one share.

3 If any man shall offer to run away or keep any secret from the company he shall be maroon'd with one bottle of powder, one bottle of water, one small arm (pistol) and shot.

4 If any man shall steal anything he shall be maroon'd or shot.

5 A man who strikes another shall receive 40 lashes on the back.

6 A man who snaps his arms, smokes tobacco in the hold without a cap on his pipe or carry a lighted candle without a lantern shall be punished as above.

7 A man who does not keep his arms clean shall go without his share of the booty.

8 If a man loses a limb or joint at the time of the engagement he shall receive 400 pieces of eight.

Each man shall now make his mark.

John Phillips   X   *Will Broadkree* X
   X *Jack* X X + + X
      X   x   X   —
              Percy   X

'Arms' means firearms – that is, pistols. To 'snap arms' was to fire a pistol.

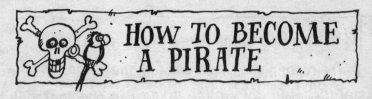

HOW TO BECOME A PIRATE

Method 1

Pirates didn't spend forever sailing the seas. They had to land frequently for provisions and repairs, and they'd usually make a visit to the grog shop (the pub). Many piratical plans were made over a tankard of ale, and the pirate crew would have been able to recruit new members from the sailors in the taverns around the harbour.

Method 2

Mutiny: A mutiny was when the crew of a ship became fed up with their captain (for one reason or another*) and got rid of him (usually overboard†). They would elect a new captain and probably decide that piracy would be a more rewarding life than carrying tobacco leaf to Liverpool.

---

* For example, bad food, long voyages, strict rules, the way the captain picked his nose, etc., etc.

† And usually dead, though sometimes he was spared but set adrift in a small boat with a jug of water and some biscuits.

Method 3

Force: When pirates attacked and overcame another ship, they often invited the crew to join them as pirates. Some of the sailors would join willingly, but others may have needed a little persuasion . . .

Method 4

Many people emigrated to America in the hope of finding a better life. They were often disappointed. Others were forced to go as slaves or servants. When their terms of employment ended, they had to look around for another job. Pirate ships were plentiful in that part of the world, so it was easy to become one of their crew!

Just to confuse matters, there were many other names for pirates.

The Dutch called them: Which in English was:

The Spanish called them: Which in French was:

The French also called them:

FLIBUSTIERS

Which in English was:

And in Spanish:

FILIBUSTERERS

FILIBUSTEROS

The Dutch sometimes said:

ZEE~ROVERS

And the English version was:

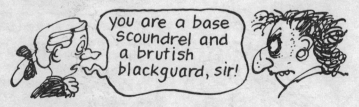

SEA~ROVERS

Some unfortunate captain might have called them:

you are a base
scoundrel and
a brutish
blackguard, sir!

But that wouldn't have done much good!

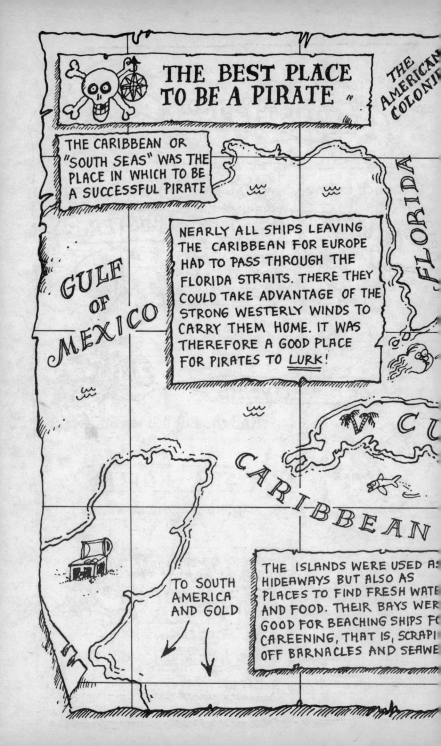

THE BEST PLACE TO BE A PIRATE

THE CARIBBEAN OR "SOUTH SEAS" WAS THE PLACE IN WHICH TO BE A SUCCESSFUL PIRATE

FLORIDA

GULF OF MEXICO

NEARLY ALL SHIPS LEAVING THE CARIBBEAN FOR EUROPE HAD TO PASS THROUGH THE FLORIDA STRAITS. THERE THEY COULD TAKE ADVANTAGE OF THE STRONG WESTERLY WINDS TO CARRY THEM HOME. IT WAS THEREFORE A GOOD PLACE FOR PIRATES TO LURK!

CU

CARIBBEAN

TO SOUTH AMERICA AND GOLD

THE ISLANDS WERE USED AS HIDEAWAYS BUT ALSO AS PLACES TO FIND FRESH WATER AND FOOD. THEIR BAYS WERE GOOD FOR BEACHING SHIPS FOR CAREENING, THAT IS, SCRAPING OFF BARNACLES AND SEAWEED

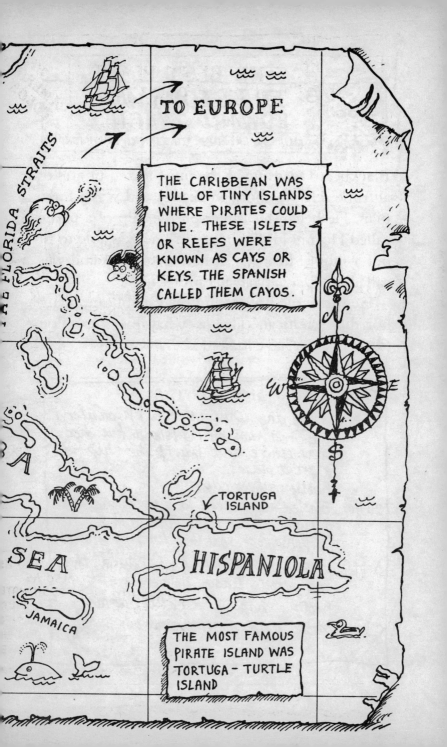

TO EUROPE

THE CARIBBEAN WAS
FULL OF TINY ISLANDS
WHERE PIRATES COULD
HIDE. THESE ISLETS
OR REEFS WERE
KNOWN AS CAYS OR
KEYS. THE SPANISH
CALLED THEM CAYOS.

THE FLORIDA STRAITS

N
E
S

TORTUGA
ISLAND

SEA

HISPANIOLA

JAMAICA

THE MOST FAMOUS
PIRATE ISLAND WAS
TORTUGA – TURTLE
ISLAND

THE STORY of EDWARD TEACH
(ALIAS BLACKBEARD, ALIAS THATCH DRUMMOND)

Blackbeard was one of the most feared pirates of all time. He was born in Bristol and was a huge man. He began his career on the ship of a pirate called Horngold. In about 1718 he was able to fit out a ship of his own. It had forty guns and was called the *Queen Margaret's Revenge*.

He then sailed off round the Caribbean, being horribly piratical. This is what his ship's log (diary) might have looked like:

CAP'N TEACH   SHIP'S LOG 1718

25 OCT Fine day. Quite sunny. Encounter'd the "Great Alan" off Pig Island. Put her crew ashore and burnt the ship — a great blaze!
Booty : silver cups

20 NOV Blasted navy sent to apprehend me!! A right pretty fight with H.M.S. Scarborough — sent her limping home!

5 DEC Bosun has toothache. Captured the "Margaret" — Easy.
Booty : hogs and cattle, arms, books and instruments.

Blackbeard decided that if he changed his appearance, he would terrify his enemies even more. This is what he did.

He grew his beard until it reached his belt. He plaited it into pigtails and tied them with coloured ribbons. He made fuses of hemp, lit them and tucked them under his hat. The fuses were soaked in a special liquid that made them burn slowly. He was sure the smoke would make him look more frightening. He always wore black clothes and liked to make his huge boots clatter on the deck as he walked. He wore a shoulder sling with several pistols and kept daggers, cutlasses and pistols stuck in his belt.

And he used very bad language.

One of Blackbeard's favourite tricks was to invite some of his crew to dine in his cabin, and when they were all seated he would take out his pistols and fire at random under the table.

On one of his escapades, Blackbeard managed to muster a squadron of five vessels. They laid siege to the harbour of Charleston in South Carolina, capturing every boat that went in or out, including the pilot. He then held the captured passengers and crews to ransom for medicine and other supplies. He threatened to cut off all their heads and send them to the Governor.

The medicines and supplies arrived, and Blackbeard released his hostages. He kept their gold and jewellery, though.

Eventually, Blackbeard settled down on land and married – although it was said that he already had thirteen wives!

But Blackbeard was restless on land and was soon back at sea and up to his old tricks.

At last a reward for him was offered by the Governor of North Carolina.

To ENCOURAGE
The apprehension and destroying of
PYRATES
Rewards are offered for the killing of pyrates. The largest REWARD of ONE HUNDRED POUNDS to be paid for the killing specifically of EDWARD TEACH, commonly called Captain Teach or BLACKBEARD.

Governor Spotswood.

When Blackbeard saw the ships of the King's Navy that had been sent to arrest him, he drank a huge bowl of rum with one swallow, then ordered his ship's gunners to fire.

Eventually, it came to hand-to-hand combat. Blackbeard received a cutlass slash across his face, a shot from a pistol and a blow from a broadsword on his neck. He continued to fight for some time. When he dropped at last, he had no fewer than twenty-five wounds.

His head was severed from his body and hung on the bowsprit of his ship.

PIRATE FLAGS

Pirates often flew a white flag when they closed in on another ship. If the unfortunate victims refused to surrender to this signal, the pirates ran up a red flag, which meant they were about to turn nasty!

On the whole, they used any flag that would help them to draw alongside another ship without arousing suspicion.

Towards the end of the age of piracy, they began to use the famous Jolly Roger or Black Jack, which was a black flag with a white skull and cross-bones.

There were other versions of the flag – one had a white skeleton holding a sabre in one hand and an hourglass in the other.

THE STORY of ANNE BONNY

Anne Bonny was born in County Cork, Ireland. Her father was a well-to-do lawyer, but for some reason he lost his business and, leaving his wife behind, set sail for America with his daughter.

He settled in Carolina and soon became a wealthy plantation owner. His daughter kept house for him. She grew up into a beautiful young woman, but she had a ferocious temper, which seemed to get her into trouble. In one of her tantrums she killed her maidservant with a large knife.

At last her father decided to find her a husband, but Anne had already fallen in love with a young sailor who had come off a ship in port.

They married in secret, hoping that her father would agree to the match when he eventually found out. But when her father discovered what had happened, he was furious and threw her out of the house, refusing to have anything more to do with her.

Of course, when the young sailor discovered he was not going to inherit the father's fortune, he slipped off to sea.

Almost immediately, Anne met another seaman. This time it was the dashing pirate Captain Jack Rackam, also known as Callico Jack.

She went to sea on Rackam's ship, disguised as a man, and soon turned out to be one of the best pirates on board. She was always among the first to board a captured ship and fought courageously.

On one voyage they were attacked near Jamaica by an armed sloop that had been sent to apprehend Callico Jack. The pirates, perhaps feeling that their end was near, rushed below decks to hide. Only Anne Bonny and another woman, Mary Read, were left on deck still fighting.

However, by themselves they weren't a match for their attackers. The women were eventually taken prisoner along with the rest of the crew.

Anne was tried, found guilty and sentenced to hang. She managed to escape the hanging, though, because it was thought she was about to have a baby.

Rackam was also sentenced to hang. Just before he was executed he obtained permission to see Anne. All she would say was: 'I'm sorry to see you there, but if you had fought like a man, you needn't have hang'd like a dog.'

A 'timber' originally meant a wooden leg but eventually came to mean any leg. Shivering timbers are a bit like knocking knees! It's more likely that 'shivering timbers' is what happened when a wooden ship hit rocks. So 'Shiver me timbers!' is an expression of surprise like 'Good gracious!'

Yellow Jack was a popular term of abuse. It also meant Yellow Fever or Tropical Fever, which was very nasty, as the victims suffered from jaundice and black vomit.

The Yellow Jack was also the name of the flag flown when a ship had disease aboard.

Tell it to the parrot

Spread gossip around, tell everyone.

'Broach' means to pierce a cask.

The story goes that an admiral died while in the West Indies. His body was put in a coffin to be brought home. The coffin was filled up with rum, which preserved the body, and a sailor was left to guard the coffin. This sailor was often found drunk and nobody could understand where he had got the drink. I think you can guess! He had 'broached' the admiral's coffin. From then on, to 'broach the admiral' meant to steal drink from a cask.

Meant halfway across the sea. It usually meant pretty well gone – that is, drunk.

THE STORY of CAPTAIN Stede BONNET

Stede Bonnet was born in Barbados in 1688. He was the son of a prosperous plantation owner. He inherited his father's lands, married the daughter of another landowner and became a wealthy and respected citizen. He was a Justice of the Peace and a major in the local militia (a bit like a police force).

All in all, things were going well for him, but then he did a very strange thing. He decided to become a pirate.

In 1717 he bought himself a vessel – he was the only pirate who ever *bought* his own ship. He armed it with ten guns, then he went round the harbour of Bridgetown, the capital of Barbados, and collected a crew of seventy men.

He did all this without fuss and gave the impression that he was going abroad for a while on business. He wrote out documents giving his wife and some friends the power to manage his affairs during his absence.

Why he did all this no one is sure. Some of his friends thought he had gone mad. Others said he was tired of his wife's nagging. In fact, he was probably just bored and looking for some adventure.

Although he knew nothing about ships or the sea, his first expeditions were quite successful, and he captured several ships.

Captain Bonnet certainly knew how to fight, but in spite of this he remained a gentleman. His victims were usually surprised by his stern yet polite manner.

He and his crew sailed up the American coast as far as New York. Here he went ashore for supplies and amazed the residents by actually offering to pay for them.

When he later captured a ship with a cargo of rum, sugar and slaves, he kept the rum and sugar but let the slaves go free.

For a while, Bonnet joined forces with Blackbeard, but Blackbeard had a poor opinion of Bonnet's type of piracy. Blackbeard eventually marooned Bonnet and his crew on an island, but they escaped, recovered their ship and gave chase. They didn't manage to catch up with Blackbeard, however.

Eventually, Colonel William Rhett was sent from the port of Charleston in South Carolina with two ships and orders to capture Captain Bonnet. Rhett discovered Bonnet in the Cape Fear River, where he was cleaning and repairing his ship. Bonnet tried to escape, but Colonel Rhett attacked, and all three ships ran aground on sand banks. Much to his embarrassment, the Colonel's ship was grounded at an angle that exposed its decks to the cannon fire of Bonnet's ship.

What was even worse, the Colonel's crew had to put up with the taunts and jeers of the pirates.

Bonnet was eventually taken prisoner. As he was a gentleman, he was not put in jail but held under arrest at the Provost Marshal's house in Charleston. He managed to escape but was soon recaptured. At the trial he was found guilty and sentenced to hang. He had to be carried half-conscious to the gallows. It is said that he held a posy of flowers in his manacled hands.

THE PIRATE SHIP

Some pirates preferred small ships. They were fast, could manoeuvre easily and were able to slip into shallow bays and creeks to hide. Many pirates started with small ships, but if they captured a larger one, they kept it as their own.

Here is a short piratical guide to ships:

BRIGANTINE

LUGGER

THE BRIG WAS A FAVOURITE PIRATE SHIP BECAUSE OF ITS GOOD MANOEUVRABILITY

SMALL AND FAST

CUTTER

SCHOONER

THE CUTTER WAS POPULAR WITH SMUGGLERS

SCHOONERS WERE EASILY HANDLED

SEVERAL THINGS A GOOD PIRATE COULDN'T DO WITHOUT

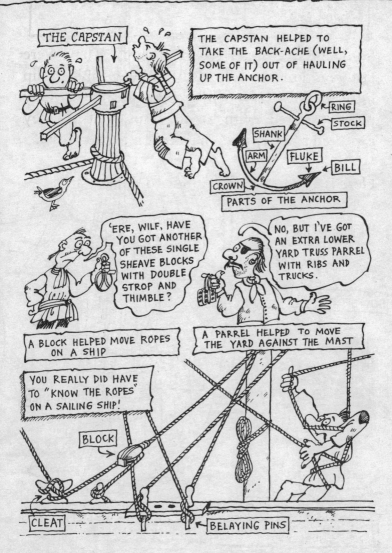

THE CAPSTAN

THE CAPSTAN HELPED TO TAKE THE BACK-ACHE (WELL, SOME OF IT) OUT OF HAULING UP THE ANCHOR.

RING

STOCK

SHANK

ARM

FLUKE

BILL

CROWN

PARTS OF THE ANCHOR

'ERE, WILF, HAVE YOU GOT ANOTHER OF THESE SINGLE SHEAVE BLOCKS WITH DOUBLE STROP AND THIMBLE?

NO, BUT I'VE GOT AN EXTRA LOWER YARD TRUSS PARREL WITH RIBS AND TRUCKS.

A BLOCK HELPED MOVE ROPES ON A SHIP

A PARREL HELPED TO MOVE THE YARD AGAINST THE MAST

YOU REALLY DID HAVE TO "KNOW THE ROPES" ON A SAILING SHIP!

BLOCK

CLEAT

BELAYING PINS

43

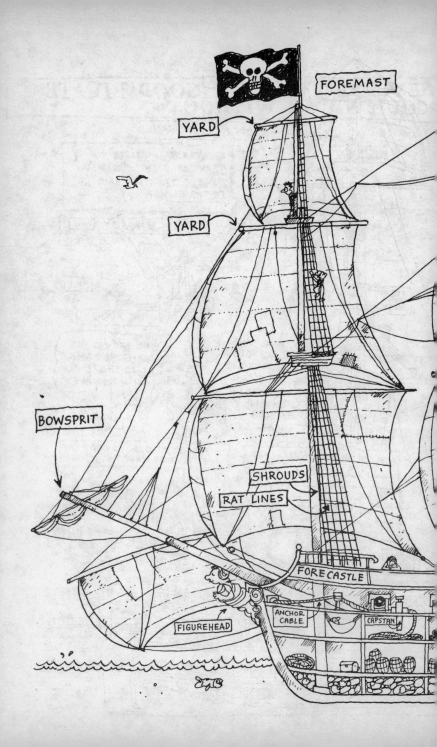

FOREMAST

YARD

YARD

BOWSPRIT

SHROUDS

RAT LINES

FORECASTLE

FIGUREHEAD

ANCHOR CABLE

CAPSTAN

MAIN MAST

TOPGALLANT SAIL

TOP SAIL

MIZZEN MAST

TOP OR
CROW'S
NEST

POOP
DECK

MAIN SAIL

MAIN
DECK

CAPTAIN'S CABIN

WHIPSTAFF

OFFICERS'
QUARTERS

RUDDER

CANNONS

GUN DECK

ORLOP DECK

TILLER

GALLEY

HOLD

STONE
BALLAST

BILGE

PIRATE SHIP NAMES

By far the most popular name for pirate ships was:

REVENGE

But here are some others:

BLACK JOKE

FORTUNE

BRAVO

SUDDEN DEATH

FLYING HORSE

Snap Dragon was, in fact, a type of drink. Raisins were soaked in rum or brandy, then set alight and floated in a bowl of some other type of drink. For an extra special display, the tops of lighted candles were also floated in the bowl – a somewhat fiery brew!

THE STORY of JOHN GOW
(ALIAS JOHN SMITH, ALIAS JOHN GOFFE)

John Gow was a Scotsman from Thurso. He chose a life at sea and seemed to be a hard-working man and a good sailor. He was soon promoted to second mate.

In 1724, while sailing from Santa Cruz to Genoa with a cargo of beeswax, Gow led the ship's crew in a mutiny. In the middle of the night they slit the throats of the captain, the first mate, the supercargo (cargo superintendent) and the ship's surgeon and threw the bodies overboard.

Gow and his crew decided to turn to piracy, but they were not very successful. They managed to take only three ships and found little of value on them. The last ship, from Glasgow, was filled with herrings and salmon!

They did have a chance to attack a large French ship, but Gow decided against it. The second mate, Williams, accused him of cowardice and snapped his pistol at him. But other members of the crew took Gow's side and killed Williams.

They decided to sail to the Orkney Islands to sell their booty of fish. This seemed an odd idea, as the Orkney Islanders were fishermen and would have plenty of their own. (Perhaps the real reason for the voyage was that Captain Gow had a girlfriend there.)

When they arrived in Orkney, Captain Gow's luck was no better. One of his crew did manage to sell some fish, but he used the money to buy himself a horse and rode to Kirkwall, the main town, to give himself up. Other men in the crew followed his example.

Gow and the remainder of the crew tried a little burglary to get some money. They must have had some success, for they marched back to the ship in high spirits as one of the crew played on the bagpipes.

They set sail again, but their ship was soon wrecked on some treacherous rocks. A few of the crew went ashore and were offered drinks by the locals in a nearby pub. They were soon so drunk that they were easily captured.

Captain Gow was captured a little later and was taken to Newgate prison in London. He refused to say a single word at his trial, so the judge ordered him to be pressed. This was the only form of torture allowed by law.

At the very last moment Gow called out, 'Not guilty!' He was therefore taken back into court, tried and sentenced to hang.

After he had hanged for four minutes he was cut down, but he was found to be still alive. It is said that he was able to climb up the ladder to the gallows himself to be hanged a second time.

PIRATE FOOD and DRINK

Today's Menu

Biscuits
Salt Beef
Salt Beef with a biscuit topping
Biscuits mixed with Beef
Beef and biscuit sandwiches
Beef and biscuit crumble
Delicious Salt Beef topped
   with tasty crunchy biscuits

signed *Cook*

today's special-
salt beef with biscuits

Food on board ship was always disgusting. At least the pirates in the Caribbean Sea had plenty of islands nearby, where they could get fresh water and fruit.

On longer voyages fresh food quickly ran out, and without the vitamin C found in fresh fruit sailors often fell prey to the disease of scurvy. The first signs of the disease were swollen gums and teeth falling out, followed by extreme tiredness.

Here are some of the dreary foods that sailors had to get by on:

Ship's biscuits

This was what sailors ate instead of bread, which wouldn't keep. The biscuits were made with flour and very little water. They were kneaded into flat cakes and packed into canvas bags. They soon became infested with black-headed weevils (known as bargemen), and the biscuits had to be tapped on the table to knock the weevils out before the biscuits could be eaten.

Salt pork and bully beef

Meat packed in barrels with plenty of salt to preserve it. When salt beef was boiled, it became known as bully beef (from the French words *boeuf bouilli* – that is, boiled beef!).

IF THE MEAT WAS TOO TOUGH OR GRISTLY THE MEN CARVED LITTLE ORNAMENTS OR SNUFF BOXES OUT OF IT RATHER THAN EAT IT!

youv'e been told before not to play with your food!

Dried peas

They kept for a long time. They were softened by being boiled in water.

Poor John

This was salted fish.

Then there were lots of variations on the same recipe:

Sea pie

Layers of meat or fish separated by biscuits.

Salamagundy

Slices of salt fish with onions, boiled together.

Burgoo

Boiled oatmeal seasoned with salt, sugar and butter.

Skillygolee

Broth of oatmeal mixed with water in which salt meat had been boiled.

Lobscouse or Scotch coffee

Salt meat, biscuits, potatoes and onions boiled with a little vinegar.

Galleypepper

This wasn't food – it was the soot and ashes that often fell from the cook's fire into the supper!

Water was usually bad right from the start because it was often taken from a polluted river or well near the port. In barrels on board it quickly became thick and slimy.

Beer lasted about a month before going off.

Rum and brandy were the main drinks (though the well-bred pirate captain would probably drink wine). Rum was made in the Caribbean islands from sugar cane. Every sailor looked forward to the hour of day on ship when the rum rations were dished out!

THE STORY of MARY READ

Mary was born in London, and for some reason her mother brought her up as a boy. She kept her disguise as a man for most of her life. At the age of thirteen she was sent as a junior footman to the house of a rich French lady.

She didn't stay as a footman very long because she ran away and joined a man-of-war as a seaman. She deserted a few years later and went instead to join a foot regiment in the army. She fought in Flanders and was a brave and able soldier.

She then left the regiment and joined another – this time it was a horse regiment. She fell in love with one of her fellow soldiers and for the first time let out the secret of her sex.

She took to wearing women's clothes for a short time. She married her soldier, and they settled down to run an inn called the Three Horseshoes.

But when her husband died, Mary put on men's clothes again and went back to sea. The ship sailed for the West Indies, where it was attacked by Captain Rackam, the pirate who drew Anne Bonny to the pirate life.

Mary joined Rackam's crew and soon fell in love with one of the pirates. One day the man quarrelled with one of the other crew members, so they went ashore to have a duel. But Mary stepped in and actually fought the duel in her lover's place, killing the other sailor.

Like most other pirates, she was eventually caught and sentenced to hang, but she escaped the noose by dying of a fever in prison.

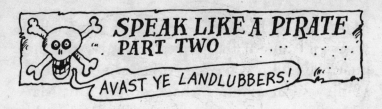

SPEAK LIKE A PIRATE
PART TWO

AVAST YE LANDLUBBERS!

'Avast!' means 'Stop!' or 'Be quiet!'

A lubber was an awkward, clumsy person. A sailor who was clumsy was known to his mates as a land-lubber. They meant he was as clumsy as someone from land who knew nothing about ships.

Lubber's holes were holes in the mast platforms. Timid or inexperienced men used these holes to reach the upper part of the mast rather than climb round the outside of the platform.

TOPMAST SHROUDS

TIMID SAILORS COME THROUGH THE LUBBER'S HOLE

BRAVE SAILORS USE THE FUTTOCK SHROUDS

FUTTOCK SHROUDS

Bilge water was the water that collected in the very bottom of the ship. It came from rain or large waves breaking over the deck. It was foul-smelling, and sometimes sailors were asphyxiated by breathing in the disgusting air from bilges. Therefore 'dead as bilge water' was very dead indeed!

Grog-blossom meant a red nose or inflamed pimple. Grog was drink, and men who drank a lot usually had red noses.

PIRATE PUNISHMENTS

For those pirates on board ship who got into trouble with the captain or other members of the crew, there were nasty punishments awaiting!

The most common punishment was 'a taste of the rope's end', which meant a flogging. For a flogging the culprits were 'triced' (that is, tied up) to the rigging.

For the flogging the 'cat o' nine tails' was used. It was a short wooden stick with nine knotted ropes attached. One blow of the cat was enough to take the skin off a man's back and draw blood. Six blows could make his back raw. Some men were given punishments of hundreds of lashes.

Nowadays we use the phrase 'no room to swing a cat' to describe a small, cramped room. The 'cat', of course, is not your pet moggy but the lash! 'No room to swing a cat' in pirate days meant a ship with a deck too cluttered to get a proper swing at the unfortunate sailor's back!

To 'comb the cat' meant to separate the strands of rope with your fingers after each blow.

Ducking at the yard-arm and keel-hauling

The yard is the horizontal spar, fixed to the mast, that holds the sail. The poor sailor was hauled up here on a rope, then allowed to drop into the sea. He could be dropped in this way several times.

Keel-hauling went a little further than this. Once the man had plunged into the water from the yard-arm, he was hauled right under the boat and up to the yard at the other side.

Picking oakum

Oakum was old strands of rope soaked in tar and squeezed in between the planks of a ship to prevent leaks. Unpicking ropes was a long and tedious business − and very painful on the fingers. It was therefore used as a punishment for badly behaved sailors.

The bilboes

Bilboes or irons were long iron bars that were fastened to the men's legs. They were usually situated in a dark and smelly part of the ship.

Walking the plank

Making their victims walk the plank was the best-known piratical trick! Or was it? Perhaps it happens only in pirate stories. There is no firm evidence that real pirates used this fiendish torture!

THE STORY of BARTHOLOMEW ROBERTS

Bartholomew Roberts was born in Wales in 1682. As a young man he went to sea and became an excellent sailor and navigator.

On a voyage to West Africa to collect slaves, his ship was attacked by the *Royal Rover*, a pirate ship commanded by Captain Davis. Perhaps because Davis was a fellow Welshman, he spared Bartholomew Roberts's life, but he was imprisoned while Davis tried to persuade him to become a pirate. At first Roberts refused, but during a piratical raid Captain Davis was killed. His crew proclaimed Roberts as their new captain.

So Bartholomew Roberts cast his doubts aside
and took to piracy. He became one of the most
successful pirates and captured over 400 ships
during his two-year career.

Roberts was very religious and always kept
the Sabbath. He detested drink and its evils. He
preferred tea and drank it in vast quantities.

When Roberts became captain of the *Royal Rover* he drew up a set of articles (rules). The members of the crew had to sign them and swear on the Bible to obey them.

ARTICLES
1. LIGHTS out below deck by 8 o'CLOCK.
2. No gambling for money?
3. No WOMEN on board.
4. Penalty for smuggling a WOMAN on board disguised as a man — death.
5. No fighting on board
6. QUARRELS to be settled on shore with sword or pistol.
7. Ship's musicians exempt from playing on Sunday.
8. Injuries to be compensated
9. Fair division of spoils.

Bartholomew Roberts.

For a while Roberts carried out piratical raids in the Caribbean Sea. Then he decided to try new waters. He sailed as far as the ports of Trepassey and Saint Mary's in Newfoundland (now part of Canada). The inhabitants and sailors fled when they saw Roberts sailing in with flags flying and drums beating. He was able to take his pick of about forty ships and 150 fishing boats.

On one of his raids he captured a ship with a clergyman on board. He tried to persuade the clergyman to become the ship's chaplain. His duties would be to hold religious services and to make rum punch for the crew. The clergyman politely refused the job. He was allowed to go once he had been searched. (They found three prayer books and a corkscrew.)

Roberts met his end off the coast of West Africa. The crew were having a drink (or two or three or maybe more). Roberts was dining in his cabin. The lookout informed him that a ship of the King's Navy was approaching.

Roberts was always a well-dressed pirate, but on this occasion he decided to put on his very best clothes. He wore a waistcoat and breeches of crimson damask and a feathered hat. He hung a cross of diamonds on a gold chain around his neck. For protection he took a fine sword and a pair of pistols carried in a silk sling over his shoulder. Then he went on deck to survey the

scene. He decided he could easily escape the other ship, but his crew were now so drunk that they were incapable of following any of his orders.

The King's ship attacked, and almost instantly Roberts was killed by a shot through the throat. The crew, still drunk, threw him overboard, dressed in all his finery.

PIRATE TREASURE

The thing that pleased pirates most when they captured a ship was to find a chest (or, better still, several chests) filled with gold coins.

Here are some of the coins that they were most likely to find:

Louis d'or	(Say *Lewy dawr* and you'll get it sounding right!) French coins
Doubloons	Spanish coins
Guineas and double guineas	English coins made from gold brought from Guinea in West Africa
Georges	English gold coins named after King George
Moidores	Portuguese coins
Sequins	Italian coins
Pieces of eight	Spanish silver coins worth eight *reales* and marked with a number eight

PIRATE WEATHER

Like any other sailors, pirates had to rely on the winds to move their ships. They had to put up with violent hurricanes or being becalmed.

IT'S BLOWING MARLINSPIKES, TO BE SURE

'Blowing marlinspikes' meant blowing a gale. A marlinspike was a small metal spike used in the repairing and joining of ropes. You can imagine that the rain in a heavy storm really stung your skin – like being pricked by marlinspikes!

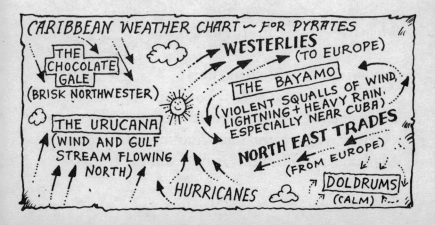

CARIBBEAN WEATHER CHART ~ FOR PYRATES

THE CHOCOLATE GALE
(BRISK NORTHWESTER)

WESTERLIES
(TO EUROPE)

THE BAYAMO
(VIOLENT SQUALLS OF WIND, LIGHTNING + HEAVY RAIN, ESPECIALLY NEAR CUBA)

THE URUCANA
(WIND AND GULF STREAM FLOWING NORTH)

NORTH EAST TRADES
(FROM EUROPE)

HURRICANES

DOLDRUMS
(CALM)

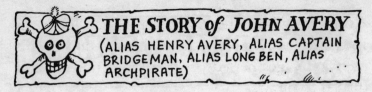

THE STORY of JOHN AVERY
(ALIAS HENRY AVERY, ALIAS CAPTAIN BRIDGEMAN, ALIAS LONG BEN, ALIAS ARCHPIRATE)

(Quite a few pirates had 'aliases' or other names. They may have been nicknames or names to confuse any of the King's men who were searching for them.)

John Avery was one of the most famous pirates of his time. This was because his exploits were recorded in stories and plays and became part of everyday gossip.

He was turned into a romantic figure, brave and gallant, and it was believed that he eventually gave up piracy to become King of Madagascar. But this was far from the truth.

Avery was born near Plymouth in Devon in 1665. He went to sea, and during one of his many voyages he led the crew in a mutiny and turned to piracy.

He sailed to the coast of Guinea in Africa, where he hauled up the English flag. The native inhabitants were pleased to see the English ship and went out in their canoes to trade their gold. It was a trick, however. The natives were bundled into the holds as they came aboard and were later sold as slaves.

After collecting a good cargo from several unfortunate ships, Avery sailed around the southern tip of Africa to the Red Sea. He landed at one town on the coast and tried to trade his stolen wares. The inhabitants were suspicious of these 'traders' and refused to buy. So Avery burned their town to the ground.

Avery then joined up with some other pirates, and the little fleet attacked a convoy of ships sailing from Mocha in Arabia. They overpowered the biggest ship, which belonged to a wealthy Indian prince, the Great Mogul.

On board the Mogul's ship was a huge treasure of pieces of eight and diamonds as well as some of the Mogul's courtiers on a pilgrimage to Mecca.

On the way south after their successful raid, Avery invited the captains of the other ships in the pirate fleet to dine with him. He suggested that they place all their booty on his ship for safekeeping until they reached the island of Madagascar.

Like fools, they agreed. Of course, Avery gave them the slip and sailed off home with his huge treasure.

When he arrived back in England, however, it seems that he had a taste of his own medicine.

Once he was secretly settled in Devon, he showed his treasures to some passing merchants. They agreed to take it to Bristol and obtain a good price for it. Needless to say, Avery never saw the merchants or his treasure again.

So while people believed the story that he had married the Great Mogul's daughter and was living in luxury on the island of Madagascar, he had, in fact, died in poverty without even enough money to pay for a coffin.

PIRATE ATTACK!

The pirates have sighted a likely-looking ship. They draw closer and closer. They are ready to attack and board her!

The most sensible place to attack a ship was the stern or rear. Most of the guns on a ship were down the sides, so the stern was not very well defended.

First the pirates would knock wedges in between the rudder and the stern of their prey. This would jam the rudder and the boat would be unable to turn.

They would throw up grappling hooks, which would catch on to the stern of the ship. Then they would swarm aboard, making as much noise as possible to terrify the crew.

PIRATE WEAPONS

Here are some of the weapons the pirates would use in their attack:

Axe

This was a long-handled hatchet for cutting through rigging (as well as sailors' necks if they got in the way!).

Pike

A pole for thrusting as the pirates boarded.

Pistol

A short-barrelled gun that could be held in one hand.

Cutlass

A short sword with a slightly curved blade.

Dagger

For thrusting at close range.

Grenades

They were made from square bottles filled with gunpowder, pistol shot and old iron.

In many cases it wouldn't have been possible to board by the stern. The pirate ship would have to come alongside its victim and use cannons.

How to fire a cannon

1 INSERT CARTRIDGE OF GUNPOWDER

GUN LADLE   CARTRIDGE

2 INSERT WADDING (OLD ROPE)

WADDING   CARTRIDGE   TOUCH HOLE

3 INSERT SHOT

SHOT COULD BE A CANNON BALL OR VARIATIONS OF IT. ROD AND CHAIN SHOT CUT THROUGH ENEMY RIGGING.

Some more nasty devices:

Stinkpots

These were crockery jars loaded with gun-powder, sulphur and other flammable material. They were hurled on to the decks of the victim, where they burst and caught fire. They would produce thick smoke and a choking smell.

Greek fire

Fire bombs fired from cannons that set the enemy sails and rigging on fire.

Swivel gun or murdering piece

These were guns with long barrels and bulbous muzzles that fired old nails, spikes and bits of crockery and glass.

PIRATE PASTIMES

And when pirates were not being horribly piratical, what were they doing?

There wasn't much free time aboard ship, but there were 'make-and-mend' days, when the pirates could make or repair their clothes.

They sometimes played chequers (draughts) and cards or 'rattled the bones' (played dice).

There was always a pirate on board who could play a musical instrument, usually a violin or pipe, and the other pirates would 'dance and skylark' to his music.

They would sing songs too. (Sea shanties, on the other hand, were working songs sung to help the men pull together on ropes, etc.)

They might even have time to take a nap. As the seams between the deck planks were caulked (sealed with tar), a sailor who lay down on the deck often ended up with lines of tar on his clothes. That's why forty winks on deck was called 'taking a caulk'!

PIRATE CLOTHING

What did the well-dressed pirate wear? On the whole, pirates wore clothes similar to those worn by people on land, though they seldom wore shoes when on ship. They did have one or two favourite items of clothing:

MANY OF THE SAILORS' ITEMS OF CLOTHING WERE MADE OF CANVAS

BAGGY SHIRT

A TARPAULIN WAS A CANVAS HAT PAINTED WITH TAR TO WATERPROOF IT.

PETTICOAT BREECHES

Fur Cap

Monmouth cap

Turban (scarf)

Jacobin Cap

HATS WERE USUALLY WORN WELL BACK ON THE HEAD

EARRINGS WERE BELIEVED TO IMPROVE EYE SIGHT

TRICORN HAT

HAIR WAS OFTEN PLAITED AND WORN IN A 'QUEUE' STIFFENED WITH FLOUR AND WATER AND TIED WITH A RIBBON

LOOSE, BAGGY CLOTHES WERE POPULAR — THEY MADE IT EASY FOR THE MEN TO CLAMBER ABOUT THE RIGGING

CORDOBA BOOTS (WITH BUCKET TOPS)

THE STORY of CAPTAIN & MRS COBHAM

Cobham, from Devon, began his career at sea as a smuggler. He had much success until his boat was confiscated by a ship of the King's Navy. Cobham was so annoyed that in revenge he found another ship, armed her with fourteen guns and became a pirate.

The first ship he attacked had £40,000 of gold coin on board. He sank the ship and drowned the crew.

At the port of Plymouth he invited a young lady called Maria aboard. Needless to say, the rest of the crew members weren't happy with this arrangement. However, Maria very craftily won them over. Whenever a member of the crew was to be punished, she used her influence on the captain to have the punishment reduced.

Cobham married Maria, and they set sail for the Caribbean. They carried out many successful piratical deeds, and Maria proved to be more devilish than her husband. She especially enjoyed poisoning people.

When they had made a vast fortune, the Cobhams settled down in a grand house on the French coast. Then one day, when they were on a fishing expedition in a small boat, they and their crew were invited aboard a merchant ship for refreshments. The temptation of turning pirate again was too great for Cobham. He shot the captain while Maria and her men over-powered the crew.

Cobham sold the merchant ship at Bordeaux for a good price. He settled down once more to lead the rest of his life as a respected citizen. Maria, on the other hand, poisoned herself.

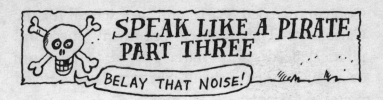

SPEAK LIKE A PIRATE
PART THREE

BELAY THAT NOISE!

'Belay' means 'Stop!' or 'I've had enough of that!'

IF YOU DON'T BELAY THAT WHIMPERIN', MATEY, I'LL SEND YOU TO DAVY JONES'S LOCKER!

Davy Jones was the spirit of the sea, a sort of sea-devil. 'Davy Jones's Locker' meant the bottom of the sea.

Means 'I'll be with you before the sail shakes twice!' (A 'brace' is another word for two.)

When a sailing ship changed direction, the sails shook slightly. So when sailors said, 'I'll be with you before the sail shakes twice' (a brace of shakes!), they meant, 'Right away!'

Scuppers were drainage holes in the side of a ship to let water drain away from the deck. To 'scupper' a ship was to sink it by blowing holes in its side below the water line. So 'I'm scuppered!' means 'I'm finished!'

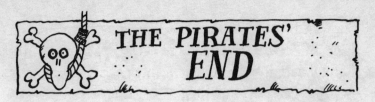

THE PIRATES' END

If pirates didn't come to a sticky end at sea – if they weren't drowned, hanged, shot, sliced, marooned, eaten by sharks, etc. – they often met their end at Execution Dock in Wapping on the River Thames. Pirates who had been tried in court and found guilty were tied to a stake in the dock. They met their watery end when the tide rose.

The age of pirates finished when countries began to have regular navies to patrol and protect their seas and merchant ships. The last pirate was executed in England in 1840.

The men who chose piracy for a career often seemed very cruel. This wasn't always the case. The pirate Captain William Dampier, for instance, was a keen naturalist who kept notes on all the plants and animals he encountered on his voyages. He kept his notes safe in a piece of hollow bamboo sealed with wax. So they weren't always as bad as they seemed. In any case, pirates, good and bad, were very colourful characters, and story-telling wouldn't be the same without them!